# MOTIVATE YOUR MAGNETIC MIND

10 Simple Ways to Attract Positive Vibes In All Areas of Your Life

**KATIE VAN EYNDE**

Copyright © 2014 by Katie Van Eynde

Edited by Lena Anani
Published by Katie Van Eynde

Cover Design by Crystal Simpelo
Front Cover Image © Can Stock Photo Inc./rolffimages

All rights reserved. No part of this book may be reproduced by any mechanical, photographic, or electronic process, or in the form of a phonographic recording, nor may it be stored in a retrieval system, transmitted, or otherwise be copied for public or private use—other than for "fair use" as brief quotations embodied in articles and reviews without prior written permission of the publisher.

Disclaimer: The author of this book does not dispense medical advice or prescribe the use of any technique as a form of treatment for physical or medical problems without the advice of a physician, either directly or indirectly. The intent of the author is only to offer information of a general nature to help you in your quest for emotional and spiritual well-being. In the event you use any of the information in this book for yourself, which is your constitutional right, the author and publisher assume no responsibility for your actions. The named characters depicted in this book are completely fictional.

ISBN:978-1-940847-27-6
LCCN: 2014904980
Printed in the United States of America

**I'm a chameleon hiding my true color**
**Changing so I won't get attacked**
**Only to blend in with a world so cold**

Poem by Katie Van Eynde

# RAVING REVIEWS

**"Understanding to a More Fulfilling Lifestyle!"**

"This book is jam packed with situations we can all relate too. It is a super easy read that I would recommend to anyone. Katie Van Eynde has such a positive outlook on life. Her words will help you release negative thoughts and provide an understanding to a more fulfilling lifestyle!" --Crystal Simpelo, Author of *The Colorful Expressions of Your Soul: A Mandala Coloring Book & Meditative Creative Journal*, CrystalSimpelo.com

**"Packed With Realistic Advice!"**

"Katie Van Eynde does a fantastic job anticipating exactly what you'll need to *Motivate Your Magnetic Mind*. Her book is packed with realistic advice and practical tools to attract some positive vibes into your life. This was a clearly thought out product made with love, and I could feel Van Eynde supporting me every step of the way." --Lena Anani, Author of *OMG Do It Now: Be the Voice You Want to Hear in the World*

### "Positive and Uplifting!"

"Katie Van Eynde's insight is positive and uplifting. I am able to incorporate her insight into my daily life. I realize that focusing first thing in the morning by using deep slow breathing and stretching will set a positive tone for the rest of the day. I love how Van Eynde uses laughter in her life to enhance a positive attitude." --Marie Catherine Hornbaker

### "A Book I Wish I Could Have Read Years Ago!"

"Katie Van Eynde's book is a book I wish I could have read years ago. I had to go through a lot of hard times to learn how to be happy and love myself." --Chef Dustin Farnham

### "Changed My Way of Thinking!"

"Katie Van Eynde's book has provided me with encouragement to change my way of thinking. She has provided great detail in how to have a more positive outlook in life. I began applying some of the methods she suggested and within a day I had already begun to see a difference! I look forward to seeing where this will take me in my life, I also look forward to more books from Van Eynde!" --Jessie M.

# **DEDICATION**

I would like to dedicate this book to every remarkable human being following their heart, listening to your dreams to pursue what the true meaning of life means to you.

# CONTENTS

| | |
|---|---:|
| Acknowledgements | 1 |
| Introduction | 3 |
| Live in the Moment | 7 |
| Positive Thinking Creates Positive Outcomes | 13 |
| Take Chances, Try New Things | 19 |
| Express Yourself, Be Creative | 25 |
| Clear Your Mind, Relax, Breathe | 31 |
| Pay Attention to the Universe and the Signs It's Sending You | 37 |
| Making Mistakes Become Our Lessons of Life | 41 |
| Wake Up Every Day with the Intention to Laugh | 47 |
| Believe in Yourself | 51 |
| Unmask Your Fear of Change to Become that Beautiful Transformation | 57 |
| Accepting The Real You | 61 |
| Frequently Asked Questions | 65 |
| Final Thoughts | 69 |
| About the Author | 71 |
| Free Download | 73 |

# ACKNOWLEDGEMENTS

Thank you Lena Anani for taking me through the steps to build this wonderful book. I never would have overcome this obstacle if it wasn't for you.

Thank you Crystal Simpelo Gilman for using your graphic design skills to help me create this beautiful cover photo.

Thank you Lauren Klaus for helping me put together my ideas and bringing them to life.

Thank you Bob Shockey for keeping me on track and brainstorming with me when I was in need of guidance.

# INTRODUCTION

*"I am not what happened to me,
I am what I choose to become."*
*- Carl Jung*

Are you holding yourself back from becoming who you truly want to be? Don't let fear overcome you when you can be living the life that you want to be living. Embodying the new you is easier than you may think. If you follow these steps, you will start living a happier and healthier life.

I am writing this book because I want to share my secret on how to love the life you're living. I myself have never truly enjoyed being apart of this world. I was unhappy and dreaded getting out of bed to start my day. I was essentially wishing my life away with my negative mindset. I would wake up each morning and ask myself: "is this day over yet?" When I look back at all of those days I was living, I wonder now, was I truly living? This wasn't any way to live. I've realized that you have to embrace the day otherwise you'll become just another zombie stuck in routine: wake up, go to work, go to bed, repeat. I wasn't living, because I was not enthralled in the true meaning of life.

I recently had a conversation with a friend of mine, when the topic of writing a book came up, and I realized how much I really would love to write one. It was always in the back of my head, and when the opportunity came up, I took it! Has there ever been something in the back of your head that you think you would love to do? Maybe you never really thought about it because you know it would be an obstacle that you don't want to commit yourself to. Are you holding yourself back from your true self?

I am living the life I want to be living and I am making the active decision to be happy. Before making that decision I was in a bad place, stuck in my head. At that point, I no longer wanted to live. I would have accepted death. I wasn't happy because I choose to wake up and make my life miserable, and by doing so I was stuck; stuck on a path of self-destruction. Only my negativity brought me to even more negativity, and I became lost in this world. I thought this place, an exterior force, was what was destroying and bringing me down, but it was all due to my self-destruction. Once I took myself away from all of my self-made negativity, I reached a place of happiness. I can create anything I chose to create. I can do anything I set my mind to. I have the power. The happiness isn't exterior, but interior. I have the control. I learned that it's all about how you see yourself in this life. You choose what your mindset is every morning when you wake up. You chose how you want live and who you want to be. You have the power to live your happy life, and be that person that you want to be.

Only you can accept yourself for who you are. Only you can start to live a happier lifestyle. Only you can transform into that person you are destined to be.

# LIVE IN THE MOMENT

*"The past is behind, learn from it.
The future is ahead, prepare for it.
The present is here, live it."
- Thomas S. Monson*

You shouldn't dwell on the past, because the past is a learning experience. Sometimes we try and rush through our lives without even realizing it; I know, because I've been guilty of doing so myself. That was the way I used to live, and it made my life depressing. Picture this scenario: you have a dentist appointment tomorrow. This means you have to wake up at seven in the morning and go to work directly after. Now you have the choice what this scenario means to you. Some people may think: well my day is already going to suck, and now I'll probably be tired all day! Now, what I want you to do in a situation like this is change your mindset. Remove negativity. There is a positive side to everything. This initial distinctive thought in the beginning of the day will change the entire day's outlook. Think to yourself: well I know this day isn't exactly what I want it to be, but I'm going to get through it and it's going to be a great day! Just changing one mindset, one morning, one day, can change your way of life, and you that'll be made clear once you start.

You are going to enjoy your life so much more by doing this. Do you ever look back at memories and think to yourself, "I wish I could go back to that day and really truly enjoy it," even in situations you didn't think you would enjoy? Although it's good to realize opportunities in which you can enjoy yourself, the past is the past. Rather than looking back and regretting, look to the future and learn to control you present. You can actually change your future by making the best of every situation. Take advantage of this.

Dreading moments won't do you any good. It will only bring you and the people around you down. If you really are dreading something that you don't want to deal with, put your mind in the best possible situation at that given moment. That's when you will get the most out of every situation. Life is happening right now, embrace it, enjoy it, and live in the moment!

Take every moment in. When you are faced with a situation that you don't want to be apart of, I want you to picture the best case scenario. Imagine in your head, arriving on time and enjoying yourself. In your mind everything is going smoothly. If you can't get to that place, you can always ask the universe for help. Just say to yourself, "I will let the universe take care of this issue." Sometimes we have to go through the hardest obstacles to get to what we really want in life. Don't think about how much work it will be to get there, because that worry will occupy the space in your mind that can be utilized for bigger and better things. Take every step and put the effort into the good, and then everything will eventually fall into place.

I used to live in the past, and it caused me constant unhappiness. If you are constantly blaming yourself for all the mistakes you've done, how can you possibly move on? If I woke up and I had something to do that I didn't want to, I would be stuck on the negativity. Being clouded by my negativity and only thinking of how bad of a day I would have deterred me from all the other possible goods I could concentrate on. I was in this vortex of negativity and the universe was feeding on that. I learned to see the world not for all the bad things I don't want to do, but for all the good things that I can do. I choose to wake up and see the positive. If there is something that I have to do that I'm not looking forward to, I concentrate on the best case scenario. Here's an example. You're driving to the city, the traffic is ridiculous, and you can't find parking anywhere. In my old mindset, if I stumbled upon a situation like this, I would have focused all of my energy on the negatives and think of all the things that could go wrong. Now, I picture my day going perfectly. I am driving with no traffic. I find a parking space right away. I arrive early and have a great time in the city. Picturing bad things will bring them right to you. Don't focus your attention on all the things that could go wrong; concentrate on everything that can go right. Only then will these good things come into your life.

Kevin used to say he hated rainy days because it meant he would be busy at work. Now he says, "I enjoy rainy days; it's not as busy at work." He changed his words and it changed the scenario.

Harold wakes up everyday dreading to see his boss. His boss always puts him down. One day he woke up and decided to alter his opinions and perspective on his boss. He started to say to himself, "I enjoy working for my boss and he appreciates me." Harold's boss doesn't put him down anymore. Sometimes changing our thoughts about people can change the way they are towards us.

Sally doesn't like Mondays because they're the beginning of the week and they just suck. Sally talks to her friends about how much Mondays piss her off. One day a friend of hers told her to wake up next Monday and start the day by saying: "I love Monday" just to see what happens. She took her friend's advice and tried just that. Now to Sally, Monday's don't really suck anymore. She now looks at Monday as the start of the week, it's just a new beginning.

Things like traffic, rain, bosses, and days of the week are constant and unchangeable. But what is changeable is your attitude. There is no reason to spend time worrying, stressing, or being angry with things you have no control over. That is a waste of energy, and possible time spent being happy. When you let go of negative feelings, you will see that negativity in your life will too disappear.

The example I gave of Sally not liking Mondays is a common complaint that I hear that all the time. Well, here's what I say, if you hate Mondays, Monday will just hate you right back. Monday's are just another day of the week and we can't view them as something necessarily negative, instead look at it as an opportunity to start over fresh.

To live in the moment and to think positively go hand in hand. If you are thinking you are going to have a bad day, you are setting yourself up for a bad day. Sometimes we unconsciously create our problems by our negative thinking. It has turned into a vicious cycle that we build and shape from our negativity. Learning to become a positive person will force you to enjoy life and all the moments you are in.

Life is full of obstacles that will constantly challenge us, if we aren't enjoying the ride we are just rushing to the goal.

# POSITIVE THINKING CREATES POSITIVE OUTCOMES

*"Whether you think you can,
or you think you can't, you're right."
- Henry Ford*

If we always think we can't, we never will. You have to think yes I can, and I will. Taking every moment in, piece by piece, it brings us to the whole. Trust yourself; hear yourself, not just you head, your heart too. Listen to it, and it will take you on the path you need to follow.

Positive thinking can create positive outcomes. You may think that this reasoning is too simplistic, and this can't be that easy. But trust me, it really is! I'm serious when I say that all you have to do is think positive; a change in mindset will create a complete change in lifestyle. I don't want you to think a single negative thought. Take all negative words out of your vocabulary and replace them all with positive words. Put up your favorite inspirational quote somewhere you look at everyday as a constant reminder to stay positive and be happy.

Don't think negatively anymore; it's only going to keep attracting more negativity to your life. Have you ever had one of those bad days that just keeps getting worse and worse? All you're thinking at this point is how will I get through this awful day. You seem to get frustrated and annoyed at the world. This is the time in which we have to train our minds to think positive. I know that at times like this, it is not as simple as just flipping a switch, but the reward is more than worthy, so it is necessary to think positive more than ever.

By staying positive you will no longer create that unnecessary negative attention anymore. The more negative thoughts you have, the more negative attention you will create. Is that something you would like to change? If you are doubting the simplicity of this way of life, you are not alone. People almost always think both positive and negative thoughts depending on the situation. What we don't realize is that once that negative thought crosses your mind, it stays with us, and that is what kicks us down. We have to learn to change that, and that is when we will see those negative situation we are faced with transition into manageable situations, learning experiences, and even positive experiences.

You will begin to bring positive attention into you life. Energy is everywhere, whether positive or negative, it's all around us, and it is up to us to decide which of those energies we affiliate with. Whatever you feel, you will attract the same back from the universe. Think about it. What do you want to attract? Are you sabotaging yourself so you don't get hurt? I used to have a friend who would always cancel our plans and just be so busy all the time to the point where I felt like even if I would invite her out, she's going to be too busy to come. It made me upset, and I was scared to put my hopes up and get let down. By me thinking this way I was self-sabotaging the situation. As long as I kept thinking that way, she wouldn't be available. Once I was aware of what I was doing, I changed it and in-turn solved my own problems. Take a look at your life, do you think you are self sabotaging anything? If so, change it.

I would like for you to take any negative thoughts you have about yourself, other people, or the world and transform them into something positive. Are you someone who thinks negative thoughts all time without realizing it? Say you are on your way to work, and there just so happens to be construction on the way that you were going, which causes a little more traffic. At this moment what are you thinking? Am I going to be late? Is this going to waste even more of my time? When you are in a situation like this, what I would like for you to do is to think to yourself, "I am going to get to my destination on time and safely." Just keep thinking it, and believe in it. The negative thinking won't make the traffic go away. When you are stuck in an unchanging event that you have no control over, such as traffic, it is a waste of your energy to be upset or negative. Everything will slowly fall into place by just changing your thoughts.

This realization made a tremendous change in my life. I am a Massage Therapist and sometimes my hands/arms will hurt after a long day of work. When I first started my career I constantly thought: "OMG, my hands hurt so badly, what am I going to do? This just means I'm going to burn out early in my career." That negative thought made me leap from one small pain to what I thought would be an inevitable end to my career. The negative thinking clouded my sense reality, disrupting myself from living the happy life that I deserved. I was told to revise my way of thinking. Now when I get that pain I think: "my hands are healthy, my hands don't hurt," and honestly it worked! I was creating my own problem without realizing it.

Sally used to say, "Whenever something good happens, something bad always has to follow it." She based this thinking off of one experience, so this statement became true to her. She was making it happen to herself. Once she changed her mindset and thought good things can and will happen to me without and necessary downfalls following up, it actually changed her life. Sally no longer sees a negative follow up with all her good experiences.

Whenever Kenny would have a practical exam he would get nervous and always think about everything that could go wrong. Everything would always get mixed up and he didn't know why. He then started to focus on how everything can go right instead, it all started to fall into place. Kenny doesn't have that issue anymore.

Zoey works at a restaurant and whenever she has teenagers as customers she would always think to herself, "I'm not going to get a good tip" and she would end up with a crappy tip. She was told to change her way of thinking and instead think, "I will get a good tip" and picture money. She now doesn't give off negative thoughts towards her customers and it has changed her bad tips into good ones.

You may begin to see that once you reevaluate your way of thinking it will alter your life for the better. The positive energy attracts the positive situations, and the negative energy attracts the negative situations. We will begin to live in the moment once we learn to let go of those negative thoughts.

We may have negative feelings about learning new things and living out new experiences. If we learn to shift that way of thinking, we will begin to see the positive side of everything. Keeping an open mind about new opportunities will bring us to more opportunities.

Once you replace that negative with positive is when you will begin to see clearly.

# TAKE CHANCES, TRY NEW THINGS

*"If you are still talking about what you did yesterday, you haven't done much today."*
*- Unknown*

Experiencing something new everyday will bring a new sense of reality to life.

I want you to be open to the new opportunities that life is constantly throwing at you. Is there something you always wanted to try but never had the chance to do? Do you find yourself making excuses not to do something you actually might love? Think about it. Why do you hold yourself back? You are the only one in the way of your own happiness. Are you scared to that you might fail? By releasing your fears and going after new opportunities, you will expand your mind. It will guide you to other exciting adventures that you may have never thought about. You will begin to learn new things for yourself.

This is going to make you really appreciate your life. By accepting change, you will see that you can do anything you set your mind to. Looking back day to day, you'll be able to say I learned something new each day. How exciting is that? By encountering new opportunities every day, you will begin to expand your knowledge and gain so much more out of life. Life will be exciting and every experience will be one that you want to be apart of.

Fear can hold us back from a lot of experiences that we shouldn't miss out on. Life is an exciting adventure that we are meant to experience. You won't want to miss out on all those opportunities that the universe is sending you. Once we learn to let go of fear, we can see that fear is just a wall that the mind creates so we don't get hurt. Letting go is the first step to get you to do anything. The opportunities of standards are set at its highest. They are endless.

What I want you to do is to make a list of everything you would love to try. There are zero restrictions, it can be anything as minuscule as trying that new restaurant in town, to something as large as going to the moon! Even if you have just a slight interest, write it down. Come back to this list any time you want. That is just the start; sometimes even thinking and talking about what you want in life can open up that door to new opportunities.

This happened to me the other day; I was driving with one of my friends to a continuing education class for Massage Therapy. We were discussing other classes we would like to take, and we started talking about Prenatal Massage. I was never really interested in it before, but that day I decided it was a good time in my life to try something new, and this seemed just right! The very next day my work said they wanted me to learn prenatal and they would pay for it. My positive thinking and openness for new things all fell magically into place. That being said, not every experience comes that easy. The point is I put it out there and the universe responded. I am constantly looking for new experiences, and I'm ready for whatever ride life wants to take me on.

Lisa used to have a lot more time for her to do things she enjoyed. She feels she never has time for herself anymore. All she thinks about is what she could be doing instead of being at work or school. One day she decided that she was going to take thirty minutes everyday to do something she enjoys; whether it's cooking a new recipe, learning a new song on the guitar, or trying out a new art project, she was going to do it. Lisa wants to expand her life and enjoy everyday to the fullest, and now she feels that she can. You have to start small to get somewhere extraordinary.

Chloe was never really into working out. She always felt like she didn't have time to, and didn't want to go to work sore, until one day she woke up and decided she didn't want to make anymore excuses and went to work out. This one morning spiraled into a routine and Chloe began to work out 3 times a week. It makes her feel happy and a lot healthier, plus she has a lot more energy.

Johnny used to look at life as a boring routine everyday. He wakes up, goes to work, comes home, watches TV, goes to sleep and then routine repeats itself. Well, Johnny really wants to get out of this cycle and make life more interesting. Now when he wakes up he makes a little change in his routine. He may use his left hand instead of right, or he'll take a different route to work. He is adding little things to his day to make it a challenge. He wakes up and says, "What will I do differently today?" Johnny makes the best of his day to bring out a little more flavor to life.

It may bring you closer to where you want to be in life. There are new experiences for you to try out, and they are in your head for a reason. Listen to that voice inside your head, for it is your higher self speaking to you. Once you do, it will bring you on that path you are supposed to follow.

Being creative and trying new things can become a daily activity for yourself that you can and should enjoy. Learning new things can bring out your creative side that you may never thought you had. It can help you express yourself in a healthy and happy way.

New experiences will bring yourself to challenges that you want to be apart of, so take chances and try new things!

# EXPRESS YOURSELF, BE CREATIVE

*"To live a creative life,
we must lose our fear of being wrong"
- Joseph Chilton Pearce*

Expressing yourself through creativity will bring peace and clarity to your life.

Don't let fear become the reason you aren't doing what you want. How do you express yourself? Maybe you yell? Maybe you cry? Maybe you punch things? Maybe you don't do anything at all and just keep it bottles up? Are you expressing yourself in a healthy way? Is there something creative that you do or you always wanted to try but were afraid to? Maybe through music, drawing, painting, or writing, whatever it may be, do it, and keep doing it! Don't forget about it, especially if you are feeling down or angry, that's when your best work may come out! Try it out, what is there to lose? You may find that you really enjoy it and never knew.

You might learn how to express yourself and feel a lot more relaxed and at ease in your life and in your own body. Sometimes when we feel angry, frustrated, and upset we are off balance from the universe, which will suck us into that vortex of negativity. By adding creativity into your life, you're going to understand yourself and your feelings a little better. It will become easier to let go of any negative thoughts.

Creativity is another tool that will keep you going on that positive kick. Doing activities that we enjoy are going to motivate and inspire us. Bringing ourselves to that peaceful state of mind will keep us on the track of positivity. You will see that the grass is greener on the other side. You will understand that phrase for once.

You know that list you were making for trying new things everyday? Well, I want you to add onto that list some creative things. If you already have some, add some more! Has there been something you always wanted to try, but were too scared to do, or just didn't have the time for? If you really want to do something, you will find time. Excuses are just negative thoughts discussed as self-made obstacles. We have to learn to get past those obstacles, and it will take us on that journey that we are destined to be on.

I used to be scared to draw, even when I was a kid. I painted this picture in my head that if I drew I wanted it to be amazing. I never gave myself a chance to do that because whenever I would attempt it, I just stuck with the same damn thing I would always draw; a house or some flowers, maybe just write my name. But today I can say that I draw, and it isn't a house or any of that. I just pick up a pencil and start drawing. It doesn't matter what I'm drawing or what it comes out to be, but it makes me happy. I usually draw when I'm nervous, angry, upset, or when I can't concentrate. The act of taking a break from your routine or possible frustration will calm you. After I draw, I'm ready to take on whatever the world is going to throw at me. It helps me find out what my true feelings are and why I feel them. For me, it was always an obstacle to express my feelings. Creativity is therapeutical.

Whenever Ashley would get upset, she would react and yell at her best friend or boyfriend. Then she learned that expressing herself through painting or drawing can calm her down and rather than reacting right away on emotion, she slows down through her new creative activity and it forces her to understand why she felt that way. Now she doesn't need to yell at anyone anymore.

Larry was always on his computer, on the internet, checking Facebook, and whatnot. One day he decided I'm really getting kind of tired of this shit, I sit on here everyday for too long and it's actually kind of boring. He always wanted to learn guitar and he decided that he was going to start today. Larry took a look at his life and realized he wanted to change it for the better, and he really did get the most out of his life.

Jennifer was always scared to cook, but she knew behind that fear was a wanting. That in mind, she also didn't want to waste her money on a bunch of supplies and end up messing up the recipe. One day she was sick of her excuses and started cooking to prove to herself that she could do it. Now she cooks at least once a week and enjoys it. Jennifer realized she's not going to let her fears stop her from new experiences that she wants to do.

You may begin to recognize that some things aren't that important to you anymore, and realize that you could be doing stuff for yourself that you love. You may learn to let go of your fears to acquire new experiences and become creative.

Being creative will bring clarity to your world, and teach us how to express ourselves in a healthier way.

Sometimes being creative can bring peace and relaxation into our lives. Maybe we just need to take a breath of fresh air to calm our nerves. You will see in the next chapter different techniques you can use to relax yourself.

# CLEAR YOUR MIND, RELAX, BREATHE

*"The quieter you are, the more you can hear."*
*- Baba Ram Dass*

Meditation will take you on a journey that you may have never experienced before and you begin to find yourself.

Stop over thinking meditation and thoughts that you can't focus. Let go and breathe. Any situation that makes you feel tense at all, I want you to take a deep breathe through it. You're going to feel better no matter what. Know that everything will be okay, you will get through this. Sometimes we meditate and we don't even know it. What do you do to de-stress yourself? You might meditate through drawing, taking a bath, going outside and watching the birds, listening to music, or having a cup of tea. All of these are forms of meditation.

The world can be a very stressful place. Learning to relax is one of the keys to success. When we are in a calm positive state, the universe is going to respond and keep attracting those positive vibes. De-stressing ourselves will help us in the long term as well. We need to learn to take care of ourselves, for that is when we will approach life in a different view.

You are going to be able to deal with life's obstacles a lot better and with more clarity. There are so many tense people in the world, and the majority of the time they might not even realize they are stressed, because stress has been melted into their lives and routines. Do you ever think to yourself, my back or neck hurts so badly, I need a massage! If this is you, I'm going to tell you right now you probably do need one. People may think massage is just for relaxation and stress reduction. Yes, but there is so much more to it. You are truly taking care of yourself. It's also going to boost your immune system, reduce stiffness, increase range of motion, help control blood pressure, and so much more. I'm telling you to get a massage. Your body's aching is a cry for help, and you should listen to what it's telling you. If you can't get a massage, then stretch, or take a bath; everyone needs to listen to their bodies and relax! I have literally stretched away my headaches and body pains. It wasn't an intense migraine or extreme body pain, but stretching can do so much for you. Don't forget about it!

Just breathe, if you are feeling overwhelmed, nervous, or frustrated, stop and breathe. Take a look at how tense your hands and shoulders are when you are doing different activities, like being on the computer, driving, brushing your teeth, picking something up, or brushing your hair. What else is really tense? Loosen it up, and be aware of it because it's going to help you in the long run. Think about what you do to relax yourself and keep doing it when you need to. This is why we made that list earlier of new experiences and creative things to try out. They are going to teach you new techniques to relax.

It has helped me so much, sometimes when I am giving a massage to a client I can get a little tense, I may not even realize it. When I do catch it, I stop and think to myself just breathe and then I begin to loosen up. It's also going to help my clients, the more relaxed I am, the more relaxed they become. I also used to take a lot of naps, instead I started meditating. Meditation is a wonderful way to relax. At first all I kept thinking was, "I can't sit still or concentrate," but then I gave it a chance and learned to understand how amazing it truly is. Sometimes I'm meditating I try to find my happy place. Then I somehow end up thinking about Happy Gilmore and how he's on the hammock and then my mind flashes to the grandma and I might get a little distracted, but then I think, okay, I'm on a hammock just chilling, relaxing, enjoying myself. After that, I can start to relax, just putting on some calming music, or following a guided meditation through YouTube.

Jennifer used to throw objects and punch walls whenever she got mad or frustrated. She decided she was going to start meditating instead whenever she felt frustrated. It let her to become more relaxed, and now she doesn't feel the need to throw things or punch walls.

Jason used to get really distracted by anything around him whenever he was studying. He eventually realized that he needed to change in order to concentrate. He decided to start taking a couple breaths and relax. Sometimes that meant he would write or draw for a little bit to get his focus on something else. Now he is able to express himself, and he is ready to concentrate.

Stacey used to shut everyone out whenever she would get upset. One day she decided to change her ways. She was capable of calming herself down by going outside and taking a walk, watching the birds, or smelling the flowers. Stacey learned that being outside around nature calms her to a relaxed state. Now she can get there anytime she needs to.

Instead of getting upset, angry, or frustrated, you may begin to feel calm and at peace. You maybe able to let go of those negative feeling, and start to understand why you felt that way.

Sometimes discovering signs when we are going through tough times will bring us to a calmer state of the mind. It guides us to the right direction and we don't have to over think our problems. We become aware of our surroundings, bringing us to better things in life.

We need to relax in order for us to stay positive and healthy, and once we do we can stay on that path to success.

# PAY ATTENTION TO THE UNIVERSE AND THE SIGNS IT'S SENDING YOU

*"What you seek is seeking you."*
*- Rumi*

This one day I was in the car with my mom and we were trying to find Ikea to do some shopping. Well on our way my mom just said to me, "I'm not sure which way I should turn left or right?" Instantaneously some Beyonce song comes on the radio and she starts to sing: "to the left to the left." Turns out, it was to the left.

Dreams, animals, Déjà vu, license plate numbers. These are just a couple examples that may be signs.

Pay attention, the universe is always trying to keep you on that right path. Be aware of your surroundings, ask for more signs. It's only going to bring you closer to what you are looking for. Have a relationship with the universe; talk to it! It will respond to you in many different ways. Start to pay attention to your dreams, write them down. If it's hard for you to remember them, right when you wake up keep your eyes closed for a few minutes and re-enact your dream in your mind, then write it down.

The more signs you see, the better you are going to feel. It helps you stay positive, and keeps you on the right track. Usually the times in which we need a guidance the most, is when you will get the guidance you seek. The more you look for signs, the more you will see them. Sometimes signs may mean something different for you then they do to another person. Your interpretation of the sign is all that matters.

You will find clarity in life. Signs can encourage us to keep going, no matter where we are. When we are faced with difficulties it's easy to avoid them, ignore our problems, or run away, but that isn't a viable solution. Avoidance won't get you anywhere. If we never face our problems they will remain there unchanged, and deep rooted in us. This is why the universe sends our signs for us to see. You are important. You are apart of this world. Now, find out why.

If you are feeling you need some clarity on life, pay attention wherever you are. Ask the universe for signs. It's amazing how everything connects. You will slowly see how the universe is responding to you. Write down, when you see signs what do they mean to you. You can look online or check out books to see what they mean, but it might have a different meaning to you. If you feel a significance, there is a significance. Remember them and look for them to help you through tough situations.

It brought clarity to my life and changed my way of thinking. I ask the universe for help all the time. One time I was in traffic and I was rushing and just tensed up, well a song comes on and says, "what are you rushing for" as if the radio was talking directly to me. I listened and asked myself, what am I truly rushing for. I had no answer. There was no reason to rush, or feel irritated so I calmed down. I knew I was freaking out for no reason and by hearing that sign I stopped before I got into an accident or caused some unnecessary issue.

Freddy was feeling a bit nervous on his way to a job interview. He asked for a sign to help him calm his nerves, and sure enough the license plate of the car in front of him said: "relax xo." Freddy knew that it was a sign and he started to calm down.

Benny had a dream that he was running from his sister. Earlier that week he and his sister had an argument that never got settled. Once he saw this dream he discovered why they had that argument and he knew just how to solve it. He looked at his dream as a symbol for himself to move forward and resolve his issues.

Susie was feeling upset after her breakup with her boyfriend. As she was driving home from his house she saw an Eagle, she knew right away that was a sign for her which meant freedom. That sign comforted her and she was able to move on to the next part of her life.

Signs encourage us to keep going in right direction. They give us guidance and clarity of our minds. You may feel better about difficult decisions and know they're the right way to move forward without over thinking things or being stuck in the past.

You will begin to understand that bad things do happen sometimes, but signs can help guide you to the direction you need to reach.

The universe sends out signs so we can be guided into the right direction.

# MAKING MISTAKES BECOME OUR LESSONS OF LIFE

*"Nothing ever goes away until it teaches us what we need to know."*
*- Pema Chodron*

Life isn't perfect, you aren't perfect, and I'm definitely not perfect. Life is all about learning and becoming who you are. We have to make mistakes in order to learn from them. Don't let bad things ruin your day. You have to learn to move on, because bad things happen no matter what. It is your job to take the situation that you're in, and look at it from a different view. You may see it as a bad thing now, but what about tomorrow, a week from now, or a year from now? Perspective could change your whole life for the better.

Life is going to throw difficult obstacles at us. The universe is going to keep challenging us. The sooner we realize this, the better, so we can catch it and figure out what our lesson is. Learn from it, sometimes it may throw out the same issue in a different way. That could mean we didn't learn from it, or the universe it taking it to a different level.

You aren't going to be so frustrated with the world. You may begin to understand that the more anger you feel, the more build up there will be. Being angry at life is no way to live. Life is constantly challenging us, and it is up to us to recognize and grow from these experiences.

When something bad happens, ask to yourself why it happened. Challenge yourself; look for what the lesson is for you. Don't let things ruin your day. You have to bounce off of that negative energy and stay positive. It can be difficult to keep that positive energy when something bad happens, but the more you do it, the easier it will get. Think of something that makes you really happy. Hold on to that thought and that feeling and you will stay positive.

This helped me realize that in this life, bad stuff will happen. It is inevitable. Everybody experiences pain at some point in their lives. I used to get really mad whenever I felt pain and it would cause me to be angry. Today I can honestly say that I don't get angry anymore. All I can do is learn from these experiences. Now whenever I have a client who has the same pain that I felt I can use that as a tool, since I know what it felt like. Look at the brighter side of bad situations. That is why they are here, to help us grow and understand life. I'm ready to bounce off of that and stay positive. I'm not going to let something ruin my day, or life. I'm going to simply evolve from it, and turn this bad thing into something wonderful. If we keep trying something the same way every time, you will always get the same results, and we have to accept change to see a difference.

Phil never used to study for his tests in school, which led him to fail. He realized one day that he needed to get his shit together because he has his driver's license exam coming up. Phil started to study and he passed his test. Now he knows his mistakes are in the past, and can move forward and learn from those experiences.

Gary started to take pills and drink all the time. He was getting out of control and would blackout a lot. He woke up almost everyday feeling nauseas and would get sick. Gary didn't want to be this person anymore and asked for help. It's hard for him at first, but everyday it gets easier. He learned from his past mistakes and now he is helping other people with their addictions.

Stacey used to lie a lot. Her best friend was starting to mistrust her. She told Stacey she couldn't handle her lying anymore, and lost her as a friend. Stacey learned that day, that it's not right, and it hurt her even though she was the one lying. She decided she was done lying and didn't want to be that person anymore. Stacey took her mistakes and turned it into a lesson of something she will never do again.

You may begin to see your mistakes and take them as your life lessons. You can keep making mistakes all you want but when you actually learn from them, that's when you can move forward and grow into somebody better. Everybody makes bad choices at some point in their lives, so what do we do, keep making those choices? No. It's not going to get you anywhere. Once you begin to see the pattern and stop it, you will understand and be able to take those experiences and learn from them. You may have done things in your past you aren't proud of, but once you let go of them, you may see that there are reasons why we make mistakes. In the example I gave about Gary and his addiction; he did something he isn't proud of but he learned and is helping people with their addictions. Gary got past his obstacles and is bettering himself and other people. The mistakes he made in his life brought him to help others with the same issues.

We learn. We laugh. We change. Life without humor is boring, so why not laugh at our mistakes. Bad experiences happen to everyone, and sometimes the best way to deal is to laugh about them.

Everybody makes mistakes, but mistakes can be turned into lessons that become new and amazing experiences.

# WAKE UP EVERY DAY WITH THE INTENTION TO LAUGH

*"A day without laughter is a day wasted."*
*- Charlie Chaplin*

Throughout life you will come across difficult times, sometimes the best way to deal with it is to laugh.

Don't be so serious, life is about having a good time; celebrate life. The more you celebrate the more there is to celebrate! Any time you are feeling angry or sad take a look at the situation and find humor in it. Sometimes we have to be able to look outside the box in order for us to understand why things happen to us. Laughter will help you do this.

Wake up everyday with the intention to laugh. Laughing can be very therapeutic, it's going to relax you and loosen you up. After a long busy day, do you ever just sit down go on YouTube and watch a humorous video? How do you feel after that? I feel relaxed, calm and I'm ready to take on whatever life is going to throw at me. That's the way we should approach life; embrace it!

Once you are able to loosen up, you're going to have a better attitude about everything. It's going to keep you going on that positive kick. If you aren't laughing you aren't living. You maybe having an awful day, and you can be angry at the world but it's not going to get you anywhere. Laughing can brighten up your day so look for humor in your day.

When you come across something that makes you angry, or frustrated, I want you to stop, breathe, and laugh. The sole act of laughter can release the anger we are feeling. When you are in an intense situation, take a break and find humor in something. Sometimes we just need to laugh, and most of the time we are so wrapped up in our unhappiness that we don't realize that the laughter is missing. You should never forget that. When we are faced in awful situations we have to look at the brighter side of it. Funerals for an example can be really depressing, but we have to think of all the good times we had with our friends and family. Sharing memories about the pleasant times can help us appreciate our lives.

I was able to let go of anger, and calm my nerves with laughter. It made me express my real feelings and let go of them. Which brought me to a more relaxed place in my mind, and I was capable of loosening up. Now I find that I'm a much calmer person. Sometimes I make stupid mistakes, but all I can do is laugh at myself and move on. Plus sometimes, making stupid mistakes make for some great stories!

Whenever Krissy is driving and gets cut off by somebody she used to flip them off and then try to cut them off in return. One day she changed that and just laughed about it and said to herself, "okay jerk, you're not really going any faster than me." She let go of her anger and looked for humor instead.

Whenever Jessica would stub her toe, she used to get so mad and start swearing. Sometimes she would end up hurting herself again because she was so angry. Now she holds her legs and rocks back and forth while thinking about Peter Griffin from Family Guy because it makes her laugh and she can move away from any negative thoughts.

Arthur used to get mad whenever he would fall. One day he was with his friend running up stairs and he tripped and fell up the stairs. All they could do was laugh. It released the negativity inside of him. He now laughs at himself instead of being mad. It helped Arthur become more relaxed and release his anger.

You may learn to let go of those little things that irritate throughout your day, and laugh at them instead. This will keep you staying positive and you won't get sucked into that vortex of negativity. Laughing at yourself may clear your mind and you just won't care anymore.

Sometimes laughing can brings out that negative thinking we may feel about ourselves. We can learn to laugh at ourselves and accept the fact that everyone makes mistakes and you will become a better person by learning from them.

Laughter will release negativity in a therapeutic way.

# BELIEVE IN YOURSELF

*"Believe in yourself, for it is only you who can determine whether or not you are the achiever of your dreams."*
*- Kishore Bansal*

If you don't believe in yourself, who will? Know that you can do anything you set your mind to, you just have to believe that you can do it!

Don't doubt who you are. Release any negative thoughts you may have about yourself. Is there something you feel you aren't good at, but would like to change that? If you want to change it, just say an affirmation. Affirmations are positive statements, you can use as tools to help you believe in yourself.

Here are a couple affirmations that you can say to yourself to help you transition into the person that you want to be:

1. When you worry about the future:

    "I let go of my fears and worries about the future."

2. When you have a hard time expressing yourself:

    "I express myself freely and openly."

3. When you are angry:

    "I let go of my anger so I can see clearly."


There are so many more affirmations, you can look them up online or make some up for yourself.

You will become a lot more confident and certain about yourself. If somebody is constantly putting you down, and saying you're not good enough, how do you think you are going to feel? Probably not so good. How about if you are telling yourself these things. How then do you expect yourself to succeed? You won't. The sooner you believe in yourself, the easier it will be to succeed.

If you want to change your self-harming negative habits, this is the solution to your problem. You will see that once you believe in yourself, you can truly do anything! It's going to make life easier and more enjoyable, especially when faced with difficult obstacles.

I want you to write down five words that you think describe who you are. Are they positive or negative? If they are negative, why do you think that way about yourself? Change them to something positive that you would like to be. Tell yourself these things everyday. Saying: I am a happy, strong, healthy person, will keep you positive. The repetition of all those things you want to be will get you to the place where you really will be those things.

When I first heard about affirmations I was hesitant about it. It seemed too simple, but it might not be at first. The more you say those positive affirmations to yourself the easier it gets. I was unaware of the power that it has to change my life for the better. Once I started using them, it brought me to the realization that you have to believe in yourself in order to succeed. I now tell myself positive affirmations everyday, and I can see the difference it has made in my life. I am and have become all those positive words I tell myself.

Harry never believed in himself when it came to job interviews. Harry used to get nervous and would forget everything he prepared. On his next interview he was told to take a step back and breathe, not worrying about how it could go wrong, just picture everything going perfectly, saying to yourself, "I am prepared for this job interview." He did this and he got the job. Now he realized that all he has to do is to trust his self, and let go of any doubts.

Kerry never was too social when meeting new people. She felt that no one was really interested in or cared about what she had to contribute to a conversation. She was told by a friend to stop thinking that way about her, and tell herself, "I am social and have interesting things to talk about." She tried it and became a lot more confident in herself. She now loves talking to new people, and goes out of her comfort zone. Kerry learned that once she changed her negative thinking about herself it changed the scenario for the better.

Whenever Larry started to study he used to think, "I can't focus and concentrate," and would get sucked into a vortex of procrastination. Now he looks at his work and whenever he feels overwhelmed he says, "I can do this and I will," and he keeps going. Larry stopped the negative thoughts and became positive; he no longer has this problem.

You may start to see that you can do everything you set your mind to. You can change your bad habits into good habits. Life will become easier and more enjoyable.

Believe in yourself, and you will become that person you want to be. You will see that you are just a worm transitioning into that butterfly. Change, adapt, and fly into the better you.

You have the power to become who you want to be by changing the way you feel about yourself.

# UNMASK YOUR FEAR OF CHANGE TO BECOME THAT BEAUTIFUL TRANSFORMATION

*"New beginnings are often disguised as painful endings"*
*- Lao Tzu*

Change can be a good thing, if you let it be.

Accept change. Instead of thinking about all the bad things that can happen when you are faced with change, look at all the good things that will happen. Just focus on that, because there is no point of bringing unnecessary negativity into your life. Don't let the fear of change overcome you. You have to replace that fear with courage.

Once you learn to let go of fear, you will focus on how good that change will be in your life which will bring you on the path you are supposed to be on. Some obstacles won't seem as difficult to you anymore. Life will become easier and more enjoyable. We get used to everything eventually and it disguises how good change can really be. Before you assume that change is bad, take a look at how it can be good.

If you are holding onto fear, you are resisting life and that path you that you should be on. Fear brings us down, and we start to question ourselves about the choices we are making. What if this goes wrong, or if this happens? We need to train ourselves to let go of those feelings, and stop asking questions that set up a negative answer. Think of all the things that will go right, and focus on that. That is where you will start to see all the good things change will bring.

The next time you are faced with any adjustment in your life, I want you to think of the good effect this change will have on your life. Don't think a single negative thought about change. If you do, replace those negative words with positive words. If you are having a hard time with that, just tell yourself, "I openly accept change and all the good things coming my way."

This let me be open to opportunities. The more I didn't try to fight it, the more opportunities kept coming at me. When I was faced with a new opportunity, I put all my energy into how much of a benefit it would be for me. When I was asked if I wanted to learn prenatal massage, I pushed away my fear of failing and trying new things and I thought about everything that will go right. I realized that I would only be holding myself back by not doing so. After learning prenatal massage I can expand my practice and gain new clients. Now I am constantly thinking of new opportunities for me to broaden myself. The more you accept change the more opportunities will keep coming at you and it will only gets easier the more you keep doing it.

Whenever Brianna gets a new project for work she used to think of all the bad things that can go wrong and how annoying it could turn out. Now she looks at it as a chance to expand herself and her knowledge about her job. The projects come a lot easier for her now and she's ready to take on the next challenge.

Connie is in a relationship where she isn't happy, but she is comfortable. She is afraid to move on, and knows that she is stuck because of her unhappiness. One day she decided she didn't want to feel that way anymore, so she broke up with him. Connie knows that she has to accept the change in her life in order for herself to happy and to see new opportunities for herself.

Aaron got kicked out of school for failing. He now has to find a new school and start all over again. At first it makes him really upset and frustrated, but he slowly started to realize it's a new beginning and he has experience now. He can take that experience and use that as a tool. Aaron is ready to move forward in his life for the better.

Once you see the change, accept it, and stay positive about that change. It will open up the door and bring those opportunities straight to you. You may see how good change can really be, and understand that it is here for us to develop and transform into that person we are meant to become.

You can change your life by accepting who you are, and the path you are on.

# ACCEPTING THE REAL YOU

*"To be beautiful means to be yourself. You don't need to be others; you need to accept yourself."*
*–Thich Nhat Hanh*

Congratulations on reading my book and taking on the challenge to incorporate these new strategies into your life. You are starting a wonderful journey on becoming that person that you are destined to be.

Remember to stay positive, live in the moment, and believe in yourself. Be that person that you want to be, live everyday for yourself, because you matter. You have the power to do anything you set your mind to. This is the life that you were given and you are here for a reason.

Use positive affirmations everyday; put them by your bed, on your door, or by your mirror. Tell yourself all those positive things that you see inside yourself, and all that you want to be. Listen to your that voice inside of head, for that is your higher self speaking to yourself. You always know the way, and remember to look for signs; the universe is apart of you and always listening.

I became that person I truly wanted to be. Listening to my higher self kept me going on that path I am destined to be on. I understand now that life will throw many different obstacles at us, and we have to take on the challenges to expand and grow. I used to be scared of the future and I only dwelled in the past. Now I'm ready for whatever journey that life is going to take me on. I refuse to let negativity drag me down to that black hole. I will rise above and stay there vibrating constantly at my highest.

By incorporating my strategies into your daily life you will see yourself in a different light. Life will have a new meaning, and you will start to accept everything for what it is. You won't feel as if the universe is against you, but instead working with you. Those negative feelings will begin to disappear, and you find yourself at peace and able to be positive in situations you usually wouldn't.

Can you imagine what the world would turn into if one person everyday learned how to get rid of their negative thinking? If we create negativity by just thinking it, what if everyone thought positive? The world would be a better place. If my book can help one person's thoughts change how they perceive the world from the negative to positive that makes me extremely happy. I want the world to become a place, not where we feed off of everyone's negativity, but somewhere that we can bounce off of each other's positive energy, constantly creating new opportunities for ourselves and accepting everything for what it is.

# FREQUENTLY ASKED QUESTIONS

**How can I live in the moment?**

Make the best of every situation. Don't focus all your energy on the things that could go wrong, instead concentrate on all the things that will go right.

**Why is it bad to think negatively?**

The more negative thoughts you have, the more negative attention you will create for yourself. Whatever you feel you will attract.

**What will happen if I try new things everyday?**

By trying new things everyday, you will expand your knowledge and gain so much from life. New opportunities will be knocking at your door the minute you become open to them.

**How are we creating the negative energy around us?**

Sometimes when we feel angry, frustrated, or upset, we are off balance from the universe, which can suck us into that vortex of negativity.

**What do I do when I am feeling overwhelmed by life?**

Breathe. If you are feeling overwhelmed, nervous, or frustrated, stop and take a breath.

**How will I find these signs the universe is sending me?**

You can look for signs in dreams, songs, animals, license plates, etc. They are all around us. Pay attention, the universe is always trying to keep you on that right path.

**What do I do when life keeps throwing bad things at me?**

You may learn to let go of those little things that irritate you throughout your day, and laugh at them instead. Humor is your friend.

**Why do bad things happen to us?**

Life is constantly challenging us, it is up to us to recognize and grow from these experiences.

**How can I accept myself for who I am?**

Remember that you have the power to become who you want to be by changing the way you feel about yourself.

**How do I stay positive, when I'm faced with change?**

Think of all the things that will go right, and stay focused on them.

# FINAL THOUGHTS

You have all the answers inside of yourself; listen and you will hear, look and you will see, believe in yourself and you will get there.

If you have any questions for me, you can contact me at info@KatieLovesLife.com. I would love to hear the experiences that you have gone through after reading my book.

Now go jump into a sea full of opportunities and let your doubts just drift away.

# ABOUT THE AUTHOR

Katie Van Eynde was born and raised in the Chicago suburb of Lombard, IL. In her free time she enjoys reading, scrap-booking, meditating, drawing, and writing poetry. She graduated from Cortiva Institute of Massage Therapy in 2011. Since then she has gained an understanding about life and learned that our mind, body and spirit are all connected to us and the universe. Her mission is to remind people like you to relax more, take care of yourself, and accept yourself for the person you are.

# **FREE DOWNLOAD**

- Do you feel as if you are stuck in your everyday routine wanting to change into a happier, healthier person?

- Do you feel like your life is unfulfilling, leaving you with an unsatisfied lifestyle?

- Do you want to make some posituive changes but don't know how to get started?

If you answered YES to any of the questions above, then be sure to download my free *Motivate Your Magnetic Mind* Daily Checklist Poster!

Print out as many copies as you need and post them on your wall, desk, mirror, or anywhere you can see it on a daily basis for that daily reminder to *Motivate Your Magnetic Mind.*

FREE DOWNLOAD AT: www.KatieLovesLife.com

Get started today and become that person you are destined to be!

www.ingramcontent.com/pod-product-compliance
Lightning Source LLC
LaVergne TN
LVHW051849080426
835512LV00018B/3159